The Ghosts of
Torbay

Deryck Seymour

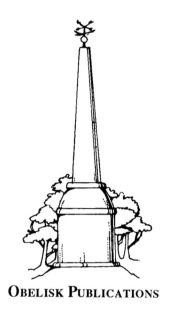

OBELISK PUBLICATIONS

OTHER BOOKS BY THE AUTHOR:
Torre Abbey (£10) and Berry Pomeroy Castle (£2.99)
Obtainable from the author at "Arlesey Dene", Mill Lane, Torquay

OTHER OBELISK PUBLICATIONS
Places
Around & About the Haldon Hills, Chips Barber
The Lost City of Exeter, Chips Barber   The Torbay Book, Chips Barber
The Great Little Dartmoor Book, Chips Barber
The Great Little Exeter Book, Chips Barber
Made in Devon, Chips Barber & David FitzGerald
Dartmoor in Colour, Chips Barber
Burgh Island & Bigbury Bay, Chips Barber & Judy Chard
Exeter in Colour, Chips Barber   Torbay in Colour, Chips Barber
Walking
Diary of a Dartmoor Walker, Chips Barber
Adventure through Red Devon, R. B. Cattell
Under Sail through S Devon, R. B. Cattell
Diary of a Devonshire Walker, Chips Barber
Rambling in the Plymouth Countryside, Woolley & Lister
The DevonAir Book of Family Walks, Chips Barber
Running in Devon, John Legge
Walking "With a Tired Terrier" In & Around Torbay, Brian Carter
Spooky
Tales of the Unexplained in Devon, Judy Chard
Haunted Happenings in Devon, Judy Chard
Dark & Dastardly Dartmoor, Sally & Chips Barber
The Ghosts of Exeter, Sally & Chips Barber
Nostalgia
An Exeter Boyhood, Frank Retter
Ide, Bill Rowland
Memories of Newton Abbot, Elsie Townsend
Talking About Topsham, Sara Vernon
Old Pictures
Albert Labbett's Crediton Collection
An Alphington Album, P. Aplin & J. Gaskell
Pictures of Paignton, Peter Tully
The Dawlish Collection, Bernard Chapman
The Totnes Collection, Bill Bennett

This little book is dedicated, with all good wishes, to Peter Underwood, President of the Ghost Club, and to his wife, Joyce.

ACKNOWLEDGEMENTS:My thanks are due to the following people who have so kindly helped me in my researches: Mrs F. Adnams, Mrs R. B. Christmas, Mr M. Dowdell, Mrs Foster, Kevin, Mr A. Leach, Mr & Mrs M. Linder, Mrs Norman, Oldway Links Hotel (Manageress of), Mr & Mrs T. E. B. Palfrey, Mr H. D. N. Reburn, Superintendent of Paignton Police, Rev. G. W. Sillis, Mr M. Trebble, Mrs Wess, Mrs R. Williams, Mrs E. White. I do apologise if there are any names which I have omitted. All drawings and cover are by Jane Leonard, all photographs are by Chips Barber.

First published in 1990 by
Obelisk Publications, 2 Church Hill, Pinhoe, Exeter, Devon
Designed by Chips, Typeset by Sally Barber
Printed in Great Britain by Penwell Ltd, Parkwood, Callington, Cornwall

Do you believe in ghosts? Of course not! What a load of rubbish! That's just what a lot of the folk mentioned in this book thought until they suddenly and unexpectedly came up against something that they could not explain, something that reminded them that behind our twentieth century façade of materialism there perhaps exists an occult world—a hidden world. It is not the purpose of this little book to try to explain what "ghosts" are. Maybe that's what you, the reader, should try to do. But it will show you how much is going on behind the scenes in just a very small corner of Devon. And if in one small corner, think how much there must be in the country as a whole.

It has been fun researching this book, and it has brought me into contact with many interesting people whom I had never met before. I was amazed, too, to find how much literature there is on the subject of ghosts, and the popularity of it. Apparently people love reading about them—at least that is what booksellers tell me, and I hope they are right. Certain of the Torbay hauntings stand out more than others. For me the discovery that "Castel-a-Mare", the haunted house in the Warberries, still stands after being reported demolished, was the most exciting; for this house was talked about when I was a boy, and its story is part of the history of Torquay. The visit to Rock House, Maidencombe, where Kipling for a while lived and worked, was also a great pleasure. Perhaps the most poignant of all the hauntings was at Blagdon Manor, where the discovery of the dead blackbird in the garden brought the story to such a whimsical conclusion.

On the humorous side, the happenings at Paignton Police Station, which hit the headlines a few years ago, must have caused the stalwart Bobbies there not a little embarrassment; especially as the old lady in black showed such a marked predilection for the men's quarters. I was surprised to find how many pubs were haunted—quite in contrast with the churches, of which I could only find two. No doubt ghosts prefer a convivial atmosphere.

Castel-a-Mare, Torquay

Our first story is an enthralling one which concerns one of those pleasant Victorian villas which stand on the slopes of Warberry Hill. Its first lease was granted on 29th September 1852 to a certain William Reed. Doubtless he was well pleased with his new home which had a warm, southerly aspect, a spacious garden and glimpses of the sea. It was part of a new development just over a mile from the Strand. Three roads, Higher, Middle and Lower Warberry Roads had been recently constructed, one above the other, their gradients carefully calculated to accommodate horse-drawn carriages. The whole district became known as "The Warberries". It was an exclusive neighbourhood. Some of its villas were very large and were destined to be the homes of Torquay's most distinguished residents. Each property was enclosed by high walls of the local limestone which were only broken to make way for imposing entrance gateways. These, for the most part, still stand, but the houses themselves have suffered not a little from changing social conditions. Some have been divided into flats, but others have been demolished to make way for smaller modern buildings which have encroached on the former well-established gardens. The district is, however, still one of the most sought after in the town and retains much of its former tranquillity and charm.

The particular villa with which this story is concerned is one of the smaller and less pretentious houses, but for all that it has an air of dignity, and there are some attractive features in its solid design. Owing to the steep slope of the ground a three storey house appears from the road to be of two storeys only, for the kitchen and servants' quarters are below street level in a garden basement which is not underground. There is an attractive terrace onto which the front rooms open; it is supported by two arches. The entrance is flanked by two imposing gateposts which are surmounted by large pomegranates. The property from its very beginning bore the romantic name of "Castel-a-Mare", and on an old large-scale map of 1866, it is clearly marked thus. Neither the plan of the house nor its boundaries have changed much since then. "Castel-a-Mare" it was until, after a period of dereliction (the reason for which is the subject of our story), it was redesigned and somewhat enlarged in the 1920s and divided into four different residences. As a result the old name has unfortunately gone. I do not feel free to state the exact position of the house, and readers will agree that the privacy of the occupants must be at all times respected. It had been assumed by some recent writers that the property had been demolished. The house next door was indeed demolished, and so confusion arose. Added to this was the statement by the writer, Violet Tweedale, in her book *Ghosts I have Known*, that the house was being demolished at the time of publication. She, however, had moved away from the town at that time and so was misinformed. Beverley Nichols, in his book *Twenty-Five* written a little later, clearly states that "Castel-a-Mare" had been restored and was again inhabited.

All the old Torquay residents knew of a haunted house in the Warberries, and as a little boy I was constantly hearing about it. The intriguing story is that a century or more ago a double murder took place there, and as a result of the psychic disturbances which occurred afterwards it came about that eventually no family would live there. There were the sounds of running footsteps, the opening and closing of doors, turning of locks, currents of freezing air, and, worst of all, an intermittent blood-curdling scream heard at any hour of the day or night. The house seems to have been deserted for quite thirty years. It was no wonder that it became derelict and eventually ruinous. It was stated to be roofless when records of the hauntings begin. It is fortunate that two well-known authors of the early twentieth century have left us accounts of their experiences at "Castle-a-Mare"—Violet Tweedale and Beverley Nichols. Their accounts are vivid and dramatic but never sensational. In *Torquay Times* for 6th July 1962 there is also an account of what a second medium experienced at the house. These three speak to us across the years of their traumatic experiences there. Let us take Violet Tweedale's story first, for she was the first to record the strange happenings at "Castel-a-Mare".

She begins by stating that she first became interested in the house around 1912 when gossip about a villa in the Warberries came to her ears. It was said to be so badly haunted that for many years no one had lived there. It was asserted that screams were heard and that no door would stay closed for any length of time. She next describes the pitiful condition of the property when she first saw it. The windows were broken, paint was peeling off the walls, whilst jackdaws roosted in the chimneys. Even the house agents' "For Sale" signs were dropping off the gate in sheer frustration. She and her husband there and then decided to make investigations. The owner, a burly builder, only too readily gave them the keys. They decided to do a daily vigil at lunch time—the quietest time of the day. A preliminary survey produced nothing but an impression that the bathroom and a small servants' room at the top of the kitchen stairs were trouble spots. They also felt that their movements were being closely watched. On the first day they closed all doors and left an arrangement of twigs and leaves by the front door which human feet entering would be bound to disturb. The next day not a single door did they find closed, but the twigs were intact. They settled on the stairs and were soon distracted by the click of a latch, and watched whilst the knob of a door close by began to turn. The door opened just wide enough for the passage of a human being, but they saw no one. Next they heard the sound of hurrying footsteps in the corridor above, but again there was no one visible.

On the next day they found all the doors defiantly wide open and unlocked, although they had all been left closed and locked. They later heard a brushing sound ascending the stairs, as though someone were pressing against the wall. They were more than ever certain that the danger spots were the bathroom and small room, and also the stable outside.

They carried on their vigils for a month or so and then were fortunate enough to meet a lady who was actually the last to live in the house. About thirty years earlier she had lived there with her parents. She said the family soon discovered that there was something uncanny about the house, garden and stable. They were moreover disturbed by a piercing scream which occurred at any hour of the day or night, continuous footsteps running along the corridors and up and down stairs, and a constant locking of doors by unseen hands. The scream was the most unnerving phenomenon and came from both inside the house and from the garden. A visiting doctor testified to hearing it just as he was about to ring the door bell. The drawing room was practically uninhabitable as it seemed full of unseen people moving about. The family were frequently locked in their rooms. Once they saw a strange woman in black on the staircase. Animals also fared badly at "Castel-a-Mare", and the carriage horse was unwilling to enter his stable, having to be backed in. It was small wonder that this family abandoned the house to its fate.

At about this time, a member of the Society for Psychic Research visited the house, and considered the garden more haunted than the house. One hot summer's morning Mrs Tweedale, who lived not far away, was walking past the house when the air was rent by the scream of someone in abject terror. It was a terrifying sound and she had not previously heard it. The house lay still and tranquil in the heat.

In 1917 she was asked to join a group which included a medium, a lady, a soldier who was immensely interested in psychic research, and a few others. They were eight in all. Their object was to visit "Castel-a-Mare". On the occasion of their first visit the medium decided to settle in the room which adjoined the bathroom. For a while nothing happened and then she was taken over by an infuriated man who, using violent language, advanced menacingly upon the party and in a harsh, threatening voice, demanded to know what right they had to intrude upon his privacy. This hostile entity now completely controlled the medium who was a frail little woman. She now had superhuman strength and bellowed like a bull. The control then rushed at the

soldier with tigerish fury. The party scattered and she drove those who remained away from the bathroom. After a desperate struggle they were all driven onto the landing. Then, without warning, the violent entity left the medium's body and she crashed down, a limp wreck, onto the floor.

The medium was none the worse for her experience, and was keen to return another day. On this occasion the same violent male entity controlled her, but the soldier immediately began a system of exorcism, and succeeded in driving away the evil entity. The medium then collapsed as before; but after a few minutes she was taken over by a fresh control—a woman. She then began to weep in a broken-hearted manner, pointing to one side of the room. "Poor master," she moaned, "On the bed, help him, help him." She repeatedly indicated by clutching her hands to her throat that he had died by strangulation. She then wandered about the room, pointing with shuddering horror at the bathroom. She next gave a piercing scream, such as Mrs Tweedale had heard on that hot summer morning, and began a fierce encounter with an unseen force, wrestling as though for her life, and calling for help. At intervals she gasped, "Terrible doctor—will kill me—he has killed master—help, help." The soldier began again to exorcise and succeeded in banishing the "terrible Doctor". When he had gone they extracted from the medium an approximate date for the tragedy and her master's name, and that he was mentally deficient when the murder took place. She was a servant in the house, and after witnessing the crime was apparently murdered too. She finally entered the bathroom, lamenting over the body of her master which had lain hidden there when the room was used as a large cupboard. The names and dates given by the medium were later verified by town records.

Mrs Tweedale records one final occult experience at "Castel-a-Mare". She was returning from a day of war work in Torquay. It was late at night and pitch dark. She was very tired and longing for bed. Suddenly she heard the sound of peremptory knocking on a window pane as she passed one of the houses. Wherever was she, and who was trying to attract her attention? She then realised, with a thrill of apprehension, that she was outside the haunted house! The rapping was followed by peal after peal of light laughter, and the scampering sound of many light feet racing along the corridors, and up and down the stairs. But she had had her fill of "Castel-a-Mare" and its hauntings, and went upon her way to bed.

The complete account is in her book *Ghosts I have Seen*, which is well worth reading in its entirety. She then dismisses "Castel-a-Mare" and goes on to consider next the hauntings at Hampton Court Palace. There were indeed many other haunted houses in England to arouse her interest and the great psychic powers which she undoubtedly possessed.

We will consider next Beverley Nichols's account of what befell one Sunday evening in summer when he and his brother and their friend Lord St Audries explored the haunted house. Beverley must surely have been well acquainted with the stories told about it, for his home was also in the Warberries. But it appears that he had never had the curiosity or perhaps the courage to explore the house on his own. The full account of their adventure will be found in his book *Twenty-Five* which he published in 1926 some seven years later than Violet Tweedale's book. Peter Underwood, President of the Ghost Club, interviewed Beverley many years later when he was an old man, but he still vividly remembered every detail of his visit to "Castel-a-Mare" all those years ago.

On a summer Sunday evening, at very much the same time as Violet Tweedale took the medium to "Castel-a-Mare", Beverley Nichols, his brother and their friend Lord St Audries were returning from Evensong. Their way lay past the haunted house. Lord St Audries, whom they called Peter, commented upon its derelict appearance. On being told the house was haunted he was all for going in, especially as they informed him that a terrible double murder had taken place there, and that screams and pattering footsteps were frequently heard. They decided to explore the place there and then, managing to crawl into the house through a window in the garden basement. They entered a room beside the kitchen, propping up the window with a stick in case of a hasty retreat. They then made a tour of the house. Beverley waited in the hall for the others to catch up with him and was suddenly aware that he was being affected by a force which came from a small room at the top of the stairs. It was sapping the alertness of his brain, just as though he was taking an anaesthetic. He shouted to the others who came to his aid. He just managed to grope his way down the stairs and out through the open window. Then he blacked out, collapsing on the grass outside. Here he soon regained his senses. The other two, intrigued with what had happened, re-entered the house. They returned after about twenty minutes with nothing to report.

It was then that Peter announced that he was going in by himself. Nothing would persuade him not to do this, though he was begged not to. He agreed to whistle to them every few minutes. They heard him go upstairs, walk across the hall, and sit down at the foot of the stairs. Whistles were exchanged two or three times and about twenty minutes went by—then terror! Beverley says, "Over our heads there came something which was not a sound for there was no sound; not a wind, for the trees were still; nothing visible for we saw nothing. A second later a cry from the house in Peter's voice, the like of which I hope I shall never hear again. It was a long-drawn 'ah-h-h'. The sort of cry that a man makes when he has been stabbed in the back."

They sprang to their feet and rushed into the house. The moon had just gone behind a cloud and they were in complete darkness, whilst from upstairs came the wildest thuds and crashes, sounding as though several men were struggling together. Eventually they heard "Oh my God!" in Peter's voice. They met him as he emerged round the corner of the staircase, dead white—his hair and clothes covered in plaster and dirt. They took him to friends who lived next door and plied him with liberal doses of brandy. This revived him, and he told them how he had sat at the bottom of the stairs watching the door of the little room from whence an evil influence seemed to emerge. After a while something rushed from the room straight at him. It was black and shaped like a man but had no face. He was knocked flat on his back by an overwhelming force and had a sickening sensation as though he was struggling with something beastly from hell. He struggled to his feet and fought the thing, feeling he was fighting for his life, and against two or three people. How he had managed to back down the stairs he did not know. There was nothing but darkness and filthy influences. His strength was ebbing fast, and he met the others just in time.

They were later told that "Castel-a-Mare" was once the scene of a brutal double murder some forty years ago, in which a semi-insane doctor had done to death his wife and then a maidservant—the little room at the end of the passage being the place of the murders. It was from here that the evil thing rushed at Peter, and which had caused Beverley to black out.

He concludes by saying that when the house was eventually renovated and inhabited "a short time ago", the haunting began again. No door would keep shut—no dog could be got to pass the house at night. However, in some way or another, possibly by a service of exorcism, the evil influences were driven out and the atmosphere of the house became pleasant and tranquil, just as it is at the present time.

Both accounts of the hauntings, the reader will agree, are lucid and unsensational. Nevertheless both writers leave us high and dry digesting, as it were, the final courses of a banquet of occult happenings but never presenting us with the first course. We have the Finale but no First Act. What had happened at "Castel-a-Mare" to cause so unusual a haunting and such a concentration of evil power? What dreadful deed had been perpetrated in the peaceful Warberries of all places to produce such a climax? The answer is that we don't really know and probably never will. The traditional story is that a semi-insane doctor once lived in the house and for reasons best known to himself strangled his wife—the deed being unfortunately witnessed by the maidservant. She too had therefore to be killed and was chased all over the house until finally caught and despatched. Another, and perhaps more likely variant, is that the doctor was a foreigner—an Italian—who lived in the house to tend the occupier who was an invalid or insane. So the doctor murders his employer, both stories agreeing that the maid was a witness of the crime, and so was also murdered herself. This latter version seems to be supported by the reaction of the medium of whom you have just read. Whilst in a trance she was apparently taken over by the maid, who was weeping, and in a paroxysm of grief over the murder of her beloved master. If we accept this story then questions immediately arise. For instance, what did the doctor do with the bodies? Do they yet await discovery beneath the green lawn now so peaceful and delightful? You have read how a member of the Psychic Society considered the garden more haunted than the house!

Then again, surely the victims would have been missed and a search instigated. Did the doctor abscond? Or did he live on to enjoy the peace of "Castel-a-Mare" for the rest of his days? If so, he had committed two perfect crimes and got away with them! At present we simply do not know the answers to these pertinent questions. I am quite sure, however, that by studying names and dates of successive tenants of the house, burial registers etc, much more awaits discovery, even after so long a time. Unfortunately it lies outside the scope of this little book to speculate further on that angle of the story.

From a psychic point of view the disturbances were of great interest, for they were so many and so varied. They consisted of (a) a master spirit emanating from the small room—gross, evil and physically very strong, (b) the intermittent scream to which so many testified, (c) hurrying footsteps in the corridors, (d) the presence of many different people in the drawing room, (e) doors being locked and unlocked, (f) opening and closing of doors, (g) rapping on window panes, (h) light, high-pitched laughter, (i) blasts of freezing air, (j) the reluctance of dogs and horses to pass the house, (k) the carriage horse was nervous of entering the stable and had to be backed in.

Those who have the patience to browse over the old Torquay newspapers will find mention of the hauntings from time to time. One writer said that he had spent the night at "Castel-a-Mare" and seen nothing. Others reported the same thing, and drew the conclusion that the whole story was a load of rubbish, whereas all they had really proved was their own insensitivity to psychical phenomena. Those who were sensitive did see, feel and hear things such as have been described in varying degrees, mediums being, of course, the most receptive of all.

A recent contact made through an ouija board stated that nearby Berry Pomeroy Castle is haunted by at least twenty-six different spirits which come and go. This seems to have been the case at "Castel-a-Mare" which had periods of peace. Nichols on page 91 of *Twenty-Five* describes the arrival of a sinister force. It is unfortunate that the study of psychic phenomena was not nearly so far developed in the 1920s as it is today. So far as I know no scientific study of this haunting was ever made, though the Psychic Society did visit the site. At Borley Rectory, for instance, systematic research was carried out which was invaluable. But enough has come down to us to prove that this was a remarkable haunting. What is still more remarkable is the complete tranquillity of the house at the present time. It is now divided into four flats and all four families testify to the complete happiness of the atmosphere there. Did an exorcism take place soon after the redesigning of the house? It is very probable, for Nichols hints at further trouble after it was enlarged. But now all is tranquil, and has been for over half a century, which makes one realise how long ago the events related here took place.

It is fortunate that there are the two well written accounts which have come down to us from Violet Tweedale and Beverley Nichols. Both were writers of integrity, and in the case of the latter it is interesting to note that a Miss E. M. Harvey of Penrhyn Cottage, Woodend Road, testified years later as to the truth of Beverley's experience. At the time she was living next door to "Castel-a-Mare", and she well remembered that Sunday evening when three distraught young men called in to see her to pour into her astonished ear an account of their traumatic ordeal.

We also have the independent evidence of a second medium. In *Torquay Times* for 6th July 1962 a Miss Singleton of West Harptree, Bristol, recalled that she visited "Castel-a-Mare" with her father, Mr Williams, two other men and a medium. Her father was the "burly builder" mentioned in Violet Tweedale's account. As they were going up the stairs a woman in black appeared from nowhere and rushed past them, whilst in the bathroom the medium was pinned against the wall by a very strong force. At the same moment all the doors in the house, which were closed, suddenly opened and an icy blast swept through the rooms. So in this story, out of the blue as it were, we are provided with an independent corroboration of the hauntings.

I have no doubt as to the integrity of those who wrote these accounts of occult happenings at "Castel-a-Mare", but what I am not convinced about is the truth of the murders, for we have no newspaper backing that they ever took place. It seems as though people at the time felt that so sinister a haunting must have been caused by an equally sinister crime; and what could it have been but murder? So the tittle-tattle would go the rounds of the Torquay tea-parties. The mysterious doctor must have been recalled by the older people—a foreigner, my dear, so what could you expect! And didn't his invalid employer die about the same time? Rather unexpected wasn't it? And then didn't the maid disappear? And so the chatter would go on until it was taken for granted that the doctor had committed not one murder but two. His indirect accuser was, of course, the maidservant, apparently speaking through the medium. But would such evidence ever be accepted in a Court of Law? No, doctor, we shall have to acquit you! But then why did that evil power lurk in the small room? All witnesses agreed on that point. So where do we get? Evil hauntings of deserted buildings are common. Is that all that occurred here? Was there no crime after all?

Hauntings at two Churches

The following incident occurred at Upton Parish Church, Torquay on Tuesday, 9th September, 1952, at 2.45 p.m. My car was drawn up immediately outside the west door of the church. I was organist of the church at the time and planned to collect a number of choir books for repairs. I was followed into the church after a few moments by Mr H. Sutton, who at the time lived at Homelands, Maidencombe— another organist whom I knew very well. We talked a while in the church, and then he left by the west door whilst I went into the vestry to collect my books. I then followed him out by the same door.

As I came out of the church a little old lady in a maroon coloured coat and black hat was entering. She had snow-white hair and a pleasant, wrinkled face; she half smiled at me, and passed on through the door into the church. I arranged the books in the back seat of the car and then went back for more. This took a very few seconds, and so the old lady might just have had time to walk a pace or two up the nave or seat herself in a pew. But judge of my surprise when I discovered that there was no one there. She had simply vanished! Recognising at once that this might be a psychic happening, I dashed out of the church to catch Mr Sutton who was just climbing into his car. Eagerly I enquired of him if he had seen the old lady. He said that he had seen her walking to the west door, and then go inside the church. He described her just as I had seen her. He agreed that there was no possibility of her having left the building again, for he would have seen her. We searched the church thoroughly only

to find no one there. All other doors were kept locked.

Here then was a rare psychic occurrence for which I had a witness. No explanation has been thought of, and I did not recognise the old lady as a member of the congregation. There was nothing odd about her clothing. I remembered afterwards that I did not hear her footsteps, but as the church stands in the busy main thoroughfare of Torquay, traffic noises would have drowned them anyway. This took place on a bright sunny afternoon. A year later at the same time I re-visited the church, but was not rewarded by a repeat performance.

It must also be recorded that at the same church there are two rooms then used as vestries, and situated one above another in the base of the tower. The floor above the lower vestry is of wooden boards, and unceiled; consequently any footsteps in the upper vestry are surprisingly heavy. I have frequently been in the lower vestry of an evening and heard the quite heavy footsteps above me of someone in the upper vestry. Usually they sound as though someone is busy doing something, and moving about. Sometimes they would walk out again, but whenever I called out to see if it was the Verger or Rector I never got an answer. Often I went upstairs to see who was there, only to find no one. These sounds never had a sinister feel about them and I accepted them in the end as those of someone from the past who had, in some way or another, been very active about the church.

All will agree that the stately spire of Upton Church forms a splendid background to the view up Union Street. We move next to the other end of the main thoroughfare, where dominating the harbour, stands St John's Church. Both buildings were designed by famous Victorian architects—Upton by Salvin and St John's by Street.

This church over a period of years is said to have been haunted by the ghost of a former organist, Henry Ditton-Newman who died in 1883. Soon after his death it appears that he was seen by various people on a number of occasions. The then Vicar testified that he once heard the organ being played, and on looking to see who was the performer, saw his late organist seated at the instrument. This ghost is mentioned

by Prebendary R. Boggis in his *History of St John's*. He says that it has been seen "up to the present time", i.e. 1936 when the book was published.

As far as I know, nothing further was heard of the haunting until the incumbency of the Rev. A. Rouse, who was Vicar from 1955 to 1959. Then the ghost became very active, and much publicity was given to it in the local press. The Vicar stated that he often heard the organ being played at night, yet it seems to have been Montpellier House, next door to the church, where he resided, that was more haunted than the church. Servants would not sleep there, and there were the usual tales of footsteps and latches moving of their own accord. On these occasions the dog's hair would stand on end. The former Vicar, the Rev. Sir Patrick Ferguson-Davie is said to have chased the footsteps downstairs one night, thinking he was pursuing a burglar. Both in the house and church a feeling of deep depression and frustration would suddenly descend upon the Rev. Rouse and also his organist, Bill Fea.

The latter reported to me that one Saturday evening he was practising the organ, but when he decided to go home a power far stronger than he compelled him to remain and go on playing. He was terribly afraid but felt powerless to leave the church, and it was a long time before he managed to get away. He also testified to a bad rehearsal one evening with the Lansdowne Choral Society. They could simply do nothing right. At the same time he was conscious of a shadowy "thing" on the other side of the Chancel screen. He and Mrs Fea on this occasion also heard the organ being played on the very quiet stops, which at that time were actually drawn. Some members of the choir felt nothing, but some did.

All this activity seems to have dated from the time when the former organist, Francis Crute, most unfortunately committed suicide. The haunting of Montpellier House applied particularly to the top floor where Crute had lived. Friends of mine who did a ghost watch there were quite terrified, and said they would never pass another night there.

Mr Fea told me that when playing the organ he once saw a figure kneeling in the front pew. After a few seconds he vanished. Later Mr Fea was shown a photo of

Crute, and immediately recognised him as the figure he had seen.

Mr Herbert Sutton who deputised frequently for the organist at St John's said that on more than one occasion he had been reluctant to get onto the organ stool because he felt that someone was already seated there. Often he was conscious of a presence standing beside him when playing. I myself gave an organ recital at St John's some years ago. I had one or two rehearsals for this, being quite alone in the church. I can testify that I felt most uncomfortable when playing the organ, and it seemed that there was a presence there which resented my intrusion and was trying to drive me out. It needed a lot of willpower to stay on and practise.

Now Francis Crute was given no funeral, and in 1958 the Rev. A. Rouse, then Vicar, decided to hold a funeral service at his grave in the Torquay cemetery, sprinkling it with holy water. Since that ceremony the ghostly activities seemed to die out and, at the time of writing, all is reported to be peaceful at St John's.

Torre Abbey

Torre Abbey was founded in 1196, and in its day was the richest of the Premonstratensian monasteries in England. It was suppressed by King Henry VIII in 1539, and the site of the domestic buildings was adapted to form a spacious mansion which still stands. From the seventeenth century until 1930 it was the property of the Cary family. In that year it was sold to the Corporation of Torquay. It is maintained largely as an art gallery. It is not surprising that several ghost stories have attached themselves to so ancient a site. The most poignant of these concerns the stirring days of the Spanish Armada in 1588, and is the story of two lovers—he a Spaniard and she a dusky señorita. The invasion of England threatened to separate them, for he was a member of the crew of a galleon—the *Nuestra Señora del Rosario*—and she was due to sail for England as part of the proud Armada. Dreading the impending separation the lovers hit upon an ingenious plan—the lady would ac-

company him, disguised as a sailor. Presumably she was slim with a boyish figure. The plan worked well until the imposing galleon was off the coast of Devon. Here she was captured by the English and brought into Torbay. The crew were all taken prisoner and brought ashore to Torre Abbey, which at that time belonged to Sir Edward Seymour. No less than 397 of them were crammed into the old monastic Tithe Barn, ever after known as the Spanish Barn. Here they suffered dreadful privations through hunger and overcrowding. Many took sick and died; the unfortunate girl was struck down with a sickness from which she succumbed. So the ardent lovers were soon separated by her death.

A Catholic priest is said to have ministered to the dying, although, as Torre Abbey was then in Protestant hands, this seems rather unlikely. So the poor girl was separated finally from her lover, dying far from home. Is it surprising that her lonely ghost is said to be seen sometimes in the vicinity of the Spanish Barn, flitting about among the shadows as she searches in vain for her lost lover? It is said that motorists driving along the King's Drive have seen her on bright moonlight nights, but I have never met anyone who has been fortunate enough. Nevertheless, here is a ghost story which survives after 400 years, and it must be borne in mind that unless there were periodic sightings over the years, the story of the señorita would have died out altogether.

The Strange Case of Symon Hastynges

If the reader refers to page 279 of my book *Torre Abbey*, he will find reference to the facts which triggered off another ghost story. In 1390 rumours were rife that William Norton, the Abbot of Torre, had beheaded Symon Hastynges, one of the Canons there. So persistent and troublesome did these rumours become that Bishop Brantyngham of Exeter suggested that the said Canon should show himself publicly both at the Abbey and elsewhere. This was done, and the Bishop issued sentence of excommunication against all those who had spread such a malicious report.

In spite of this anathema, however, tongues still wagged. It was now said that the man produced was not Symon at all but someone disguised to resemble him. As proof of this the headless ghost of the real Symon is said to be seen galloping along the avenues which lead to the Abbey, riding a ghostly horse which is blind. I have not heard of anyone who has seen this phenomenon, but it is significant that the story has persisted for six centuries.

Lady Cary

Another ghost of Torre Abbey is that of Lady Cary, who has been seen driving down the avenue leading to the Abbey in a carriage and pair, with a driver and footman behind. The lights of the carriage are brilliant, and illuminate the lady who is dressed for a ball. She smiles happily as she drives past at a full gallop, but quite silently. Two young women out for a late walk saw her quite recently, actually standing aside to let the carriage pass, but as it drew near it vanished.

On 6th May 1968, Mr Lee, at that time Curator of Torre Abbey, told me that he sometimes heard footsteps in the long gallery there. His wife has also heard them. A careful check on each occasion has revealed no one. When working alone in his office Mr Lee often felt he was not alone. A member of a learned psychic society once told him that there is a very evil influence there, and that murder had been committed long, long ago.

As Mr Lee was seeing me out, at the top of the stairway in the Abbot's Tower, I was remarking what a pity it was that we could not see back in time, and that if I were allowed to see one event I would choose the night when the mob broke into the Abbey in the fourteenth century during the trouble caused by Prior de Coteleforde. We were standing just inside the door, and at that moment we saw the latch of the heavy door lifted up, whilst the door swung violently open and as suddenly slammed itself in our faces. This was at about dusk on a calm, still evening with not a breath of wind. No one could have come up the flight of stairs and then got away again without our seeing them. Yet we distinctly saw the latch move.

St Marychurch

St Marychurch was a Saxon settlement and on the hilltop, high above the sea; there has been habitation from the earliest times. The foundation of the church, too, is of great antiquity, the very name stressing the importance of the site as an early outpost of Christianity in a pagan land. It is therefore strange that there are few old houses in St Marychurch; but when the Victorian main street was constructed, it stood on ground which had been built on again and again. Small wonder, therefore, that quite a few houses, especially in the Park Road area, have their little ghosts. Nothing spectacular, maybe, but odd reports of figures seen from time to time, of ornaments moving on their own, of footsteps heard at times, of curtains being lifted and the like. One old lady, who wishes to remain anonymous, actually saw her cat lifted bodily into the air and fondled by unseen hands—puss not objecting in the least!

Before leaving St Marychurch, mention must be made of a story quoted in the *Transactions of the Devonshire Association*, Vol. 64 (1932) page 159. It runs like this:-

> At the time of the Spanish Armada when the crew of the captured galleon were imprisoned in the barn at Torre Abbey they were eventually marched away to other prisons. They are said to have made an attempt to break away and escape to the sea. There was fighting in Westhill Lane where one prisoner was killed. Ever since then the ghost of a Spanish woman wearing a mantilla is reported to have been seen from time to time searching for her husband. In quite recent times you may read in *The*

Historical Survey of Babbacombe and St Marychurch how Great Uncle Leaman arrived home one night looking as white as a sheet and shaking from head to foot. He had seen the ghost of a Spanish lady in her mantilla cross Chatto Road near Dower Road. Unfortunately there is no possibility of verifying this report and no more sightings are known.

Torquay has but few buildings which date back to mediaeval times—Cockington Court is one of them. Like Torre Abbey it is only fitting that it should have its ghost.

Cockington Court

Cockington is far too well known as a tourist attraction to need any introduction here. Cockington Court was probably built on the site of a Saxon manor house for the manor is mentioned in the Domesday Survey. The lordship of the manor descended through three principal families, the de Cokyntons, the Carys and the Mallocks. The latter family eventually sold out to the Corporation. It is not surprising that so old a house has its ghosts.

As a young girl, my wife, then Hazel Charlesworth, resided with her parents at Cockington Court for about seven years; they rented the house from the Mallocks.

They were troubled by the ghost of a Cavalier, who was always dressed in black and wore a tall hat. He had an evil face and was altogether a sinister figure who seemed to bode no good. It was said that he was one of the Cary family. So disturbed were the household by this unwelcome gentleman that it was decided to have him exorcised. A day was arranged for the ceremony, and when it began much consternation was caused by the appearance of the Cavalier himself. He was clearly seen by everyone present. He mocked at the proceedings and actually spat at the officiating clergyman. He was never seen again, however.

Most people will agree that for sheer nuisance value you can't beat a poltergeist. So to read about one we move now from the peace of Cockington to just an ordinary house in Torquay.

On 21st October 1957 Paul Craddock, then a youth of 19, who had been in my church choir for several years, was sitting in an arm chair in his home, 242 Teignmouth Road, Torquay. He had in his hand a cup of coffee. As he lifted the cup to drink, it was taken from his grasp, rose six inches into the air, and then turned upside down, crashing into the saucer which was in his lap. The coffee was, of course, spilled all over him. There had been no jerking of his arm—the cup simply left his hand.

In the same house, one night a week or two later, his grandfather had just gone up to bed at about midnight, when he heard three distinct knocks on his bedroom door. He was rather surprised, as he knew that the rest of the household had retired. He went to the door and opened it. There was no one there. Half an hour later the same thing happened with the same result.

His daughter, during the same week, was just about to get into bed one night when she heard the sound of heavy breathing coming from her bed. Hurriedly switching on the light again she went to the bed to reassure herself that there was no one in it. Of course there was not, but the sound continued. Summoning all her courage, she switched off the light and got into bed. Whereupon the sound ceased.

The Ghost Car

Ghosts of cars are by no means rare. I have more than once read of drivers being blinded by the lights of an oncoming car, only to find it disappear just at the moment when a head-on crash seemed inevitable.

In August 1978 Mrs T. E. B. Palfrey related to me how a few months previously she and her husband were driving down towards Teignmouth from the Golf Course on Haldon. As the road descends there is soon a junction with a lane which comes in from the left. Any driver going towards Teignmouth has to make a sharp U turn, halting as he joins the major road. As Mrs Palfrey approached this junction, she was suddenly conscious of a car coming in from the lane on her left. The car was a white one, and instead of stopping, took the U turn right in front of her, causing her to brake violently. It proceeded a short distance towards Teignmouth and then turned right into what the Palfreys imagined to be a drive. They both had a shock, however, when they reached the spot for there was no drive, nothing but an unbroken thick hedge. Yet they had both seen the white car turn right and disappear.

There follows next the story of a long since vanished country house which stood at Shiphay Collaton, in the days when all that was to be seen there was the church and school and a thatched cottage or two. All around were green fields and hedges thick with primroses in springtime.

Cadewell House, Shiphay Collaton

Cadewell House was an early nineteenth century house, standing in several acres of grounds, and approached by a long drive. It was demolished, I believe, round about 1945-50 and the estate built over.

My wife once related to me how back in the 1930s she and her mother, Mrs Charlesworth, went there one winter's afternoon to tea with Mrs Chapman, a widow, who lived at Cadewell with her sister, Miss Gray. The latter at the time was ill in bed, and expecting the doctor. After tea my wife looked out of the window and saw the headlamps of a vehicle approaching. It was now dark and she immediately went outside to put on the sidelights of her car. As she went the lights approached and to her amazement she saw not a car, but an old fashioned coach drawn by four black horses which was coming towards her at a brisk pace. The horses were sweating and foaming at the mouth, and she could hear the sound of their laboured breathing, and the crunch of the wheels on the gravel. To her surprise the carriage, which was driven by a hunched-up coachman, did not swing round the curve of the drive but drove straight into a rhododendron bush where it abruptly disappeared.

It was some time before my wife was sufficiently composed to go back into the house; when she did so she said nothing of what she had seen, though enquiries were made as to her agitated appearance. Later she told her mother of her experience. Mrs Charlesworth had heard before of the appearance of a phantom coach and four in the family; and it always presaged ill fortune. In this case within a very short time Miss Gray died, and soon after, quite unexpectedly, Mrs Chapman herself. Her son was unable to maintain Cadewell House, so it was sold and the estate built over. For that family it was the end of an era.

No one but my wife saw the phantom coach, although those in the drawing-room saw its lights approaching.

Rudyard Kipling and Rock House

In the year 1896 Rudyard Kipling and his family came to Devon, taking a house in the country on the outskirts of Torquay. This was Rock House, Maidencombe, a fine villa with spacious rooms and a glorious view of Lyme Bay. It stands in 25 acres of land which sweeps picturesquely down to the sea. The house stood, and indeed still does, in unspoilt country, and one would have thought that Kipling would have found here an ideal haven where he could write in surroundings of the greatest tranquillity. He stood in need of soothing influences just at that time, for the family had just returned to England from Vermont, where a troublesome lawsuit had stirred up rancour and strong feeling against him. The result was that within three months he quit America, returning to England to nurse his wounded pride.

Rock House, however, proved a great disappointment, for the Kiplings all felt it to be haunted—not that they ever saw or heard anything strange. It was just that a dark spirit of brooding melancholy hung over the place, causing deep depression. On page 134 of *Something of Myself* Kipling says of the house, "It caused a gathering blackness of mind and sorrow of heart in those who came under its roof." Its strength must indeed have been formidable because it is still remembered in old families at St Marychurch that Kipling would sometimes come and stay there in a hotel for a few days, rather than endure the "thing" which oppressed him in his own house. No doubt he tried means of ridding the house of its sinister presence but failed completely, for after only two years he and his family left Rock House for good. No doubt just at this time he was in unusually low spirits after the flight from Vermont, and so was in no state to combat this evil thing. That it affected him deeply even after he had left is proved by his story, *The House Surgeon*, written a few years later.

Here a similar situation is introduced, but in this case the owner of the house discovers the cause of the depression—a suspected suicide, thought to have been committed by a woman who fell from an upstairs window with a particularly low sill. She died from the fall, her sister being convinced that it was a case of suicide. She could not forgive her for this, and it was her attitude which prevented the dead woman from "passing on" and caused the haunting. The owner of the house discovers by an odd chance that the occurrence was not suicide, but an accident. The sister accepts this, and the haunting immediately ceases.

At Rock House there is a low sill in one of the upstairs rooms. Did Kipling, perhaps, discover that a suicide had taken place there? In the story the house owner removes the cause of the haunting, becoming as it were a "surgeon", hence its odd title.

In the case of Rock House, however, after almost a century, the haunting, though maybe not so virulent, is still there. This is now the home of Mrs R. B. Christmas, and here I was courteously received by Mrs Christmas who told me that she and her family have lived there for over thirty years. The feeling of gloom and depression will descend without warning, but she loves the house in spite of it and will not let it get on top of her. There are also a few places in the spacious grounds which she feels to be "uncomfortable". The study is said to be abnormally cold at times, and her daughter notices another cold spot sometimes at the foot of the staircase. Her son feels that the house is definitely haunted. Mrs Christmas considers that in Kipling's time the house was much more hemmed in by trees and tall yew hedges which may have added to the feeling of oppression. One more haunting must be mentioned and this is an occasional aroma of tobacco which is quite unaccountable in a household of non-smokers. In spite of its hauntings Rock House strikes one as a happy home, and it was a pleasure to visit so fine a house in such a splendid setting.

The small, intimate churchyards of country churches often have their ghosts, but it is seldom that a large cemetery can boast of one. However, strictly speaking the occult happenings next to be described took place outside the boundary wall of the cemetery.

Torquay Cemetery

Next to Torquay Cemetery are the premises of Barton Industries where there is a camera workshop. The *Herald Express* for 12th September 1979 reported that the proprietor, David Rose, stated that he was subject to paranormal activities in his workshop when working late. On one occasion the door burst open of its own accord "with hellish force". The handle struck the wall so hard that it caused a hole in the plaster of the wall. One night Mr Rose left his workshop to get a cup of coffee, locking the door as he did so. On his return he heard his dog which had been in the workshop, whimpering. It was in another storeroom which was cluttered up with timber. Yet the door to the workshop was still locked.

On another occasion Mr Rose was mending a camera on which two tapes had to be stuck in a certain position after being rolled over the roller. If not properly glued the camera would not work. He glued one tape and went downstairs whilst it dried, locking the door. On returning he found to his surprise that the second tape had been stuck in exactly the right position all ready to be fixed.

Several times he has felt a hand placed lightly on his shoulder. When driving home one night he saw a figure standing on the kerb—a short stocky man in a dark suit and wearing a trilby hat. When he braked the figure vanished. On describing this figure to a friend, he thought it might be a Mr Llewellyn, a master baker who had worked nearby. Mr Rose's father was also a master baker, so was Mr Llewellyn trying to communicate something?

The Ghost of a Black Cat

It is a pleasure to record so charming a ghost as that of a cat; but three people vouched for the story of this one.

Ghosts of animals are not nearly so common as those of human beings, and their existence leads to speculation as to whether animals do indeed survive death. At Berry Pomeroy Castle, for instance, the ghosts of two different dogs have been reported—one quite recently. In January 1982 there was a newspaper report of a small, sleek, black cat which appeared in the house of Mr & Mrs Wess of Lower Thurlow Road, Torquay. Mrs Wess stated that it would be seen sitting on the landing and that when it saw her it would stretch itself, run forward by her ankles and promptly disappear. If she moved it would vanish into the stairs. Her daughter, Tamsin, also saw it, but Mr Wess was sceptical until one day he was in the house alone. As he climbed the stairs the cat suddenly ran in front of him. It was friendly and they talked to it. The house is now in different hands and puss is seen no more.

The Hansom Cab Restaurant

Beacon Terrace, Torquay, consists of a row of elegant houses which are some of the earliest buildings in the town. As they climb the steep hill from the harbour they contribute much to the environment. They date from the early nineteenth century. On the lower floor of one of these houses was the Hansom Cab Restaurant—its title

blending happily with the style of the terrace. Whilst seated at a table in this restaurant in August 1982, George Tennant, a visitor from Glasgow, had a most unexpected psychic experience for he saw the ghost of a sailor of Napoleonic times, standing not three feet away. He was about 5 feet 3 inches in height, and dressed in a blue cutaway jacket with buttons and tight, cream trousers. He was there for about a quarter of an hour. His head and left eye were heavily bandaged. Mr Tennant was looking at him sideways on, but each time he turned his head to look straight at him he began to fade. He just stood there with his hands to his side. Neither Mrs Tennant nor anyone else in the restaurant saw him.

As the houses round the harbour were specifically built for the families of naval officers who came to Torquay during the Napoleonic wars, the probability of a naval family living in Beacon Terrace is feasible. The bandaged eye suggests that the sailor had been in action and was on sick leave.

A Haunting at Ellacombe

A house where a suicide has been committed often tends to be haunted, and that may have been the origin of strange happenings at a house in Ellacombe.

It was reported in the *Herald Express* for 13th June 1986 that there was a haunting in Ellacombe Road at one of the terrace houses. A former occupant, Mrs Cynthia Elliott, who was an adopted child, was brought up there by her foster parents and stated that she was accustomed to seeing visions there and on one occasion an angel. Mr Elliott once heard footsteps on the landing. On going out of his room to see who was there he saw no one, but all the pictures on the walls were askew and the dog was howling. Mrs Elliott later moved away from the house which was occupied next by a Mrs Freda Adnams. She stated that she felt the house to be creepy, and a teacher whom she once accommodated, would not sleep in the front bedroom. Her brother, who came from Australia on a visit, only stayed three nights because he felt that there was a spirit of evil there. Mrs Adnams said that she once felt that a force was trying to keep her in the bathroom, and when she tried to open the door something was pulling against her on the other side. She was kept there a long time, and in the end she begged the "ghost" force to let her out, which it did. On another occasion she felt hands pushing her up the stairs from behind. It was a common occurrence at night to hear footsteps coming up the stairs. They would reach her door, come into the room, and walk to the bed-side table and put something down on it and then go away. She would often find pictures on the walls turned back to front. Various visitors saw a figure standing by the front window upstairs. Two dogs visited the house frequently with their mistress. Whilst one was quite happy there, the other cowered in a corner the whole time and went frantic if left alone.

One night Mrs Adnams awoke to feel that there was something very evil in the room, at the same time the door flew open and something rushed in. But it was driven out by another personality which she sensed to be her dead husband. He drove the evil presence away and it was never felt again. The cause of the haunting was probably a suicide which happened some years ago in the front room. At the present time the owner has nothing to report.

Babbacombe

Mrs Foster of Walls Hill, Babbacombe, Torquay, told me, in September 1971, several stories of the ghosts which haunt her house. The first was of an elderly gentleman whom she has seen on several occasions. He sits beside the fire in an armchair, smoking a pipe and reading contentedly. At his feet are two spaniels; he is dressed in the style of the 1920s. She has enquired of older residents who have identified him as the Marquis of Hartington, who used to live in the house.

Mrs Foster also related that whilst she was looking over the house before residing there, she was tapped on the shoulder, and a voice said, "You will take it, my dear, won't you?" On turning round she beheld a little old lady, who immediately vanished.

A Doctor and Mrs Minifie once lived in this house. The doctor, identified by former patients who remember him, is also seen, but is mostly heard walking up and down the stairs at all hours of the day and night. Mrs Minifie, who was a little strange in the head before she died, is seen frequently. She fusses about the house. Once a young man, a visitor, appeared at breakfast looking as white as a sheet. On being asked if he felt ill, he replied that he had been woken up by a little old lady who pulled back the bedclothes and said, "Hurry up! Hurry up!" As she spoke she disappeared. This is typical of Mrs Minifie.

At the bottom of the garden was a Coastguard's lookout post—the building connected with it has long since disappeared. In this part of the garden all the family feel that they are being watched by something hostile. Mrs Foster and some of the children have seen an old coastguard of rather fearsome appearance with a telescope under his arm. The dog evidently sees him too, for he once growled and went for him—only to fall over ignominiously on reaching the apparition, which was, of course, not flesh and blood.

Mrs Foster also said that whenever she is ill or in trouble she sees a lady, once a member of the family, who sits beside her and soothes her. Once when very ill, this apparition asked her to leave her body and come with her. Mrs Foster was then conscious of looking down upon her own body lying on the bed. She accompanied her companion down the stairs and through the living room. There she saw her husband, but could not attract his attention. Her companion then passed through the window, which was closed, asking her to do the same; but she could not get through. The next moment she regained consciousness in bed. She was fully recovered next day, related to her husband what had happened, and on looking at the place where she was invited to pass through the window, was amazed to see her own finger prints high up on the pane.

Mrs Foster is, of course, psychic and so particularly receptive to occult power.

From another source I learnt that Doctor Minifie used to climb the stairs with difficulty, and the exertion caused him to breathe heavily. He has frequently been seen bending over the children's beds, usually at about 10 p.m. There have been alterations in this room and a door which is no longer there is heard to open and shut.

Mrs Minifie used to follow Mrs Foster about when she was doing housework, telling her to do it properly. It would be interesting to delve into the past of this doctor and his wife in the hope of discovering some reason why they could not rest in peace!

Also at Babbacombe, so I am told by Mrs Edna White, there is a house in Seaton Close which was haunted. This is all the more odd as the houses there were only built in 1963 and so have but a short history. A family who lived there for a couple of years stated to Mrs White that they were constantly finding rusty pins stuck in curtains and the paintwork of windows. At times there was also a strong odour of fish. They would also see the ghost of a young girl of about 17 who had very red hands. She was always worried and looking for her little brother who was lost and she feared had been done away with. All this she managed to impart to them. There was also the ghost which the children saw of a tall, thin, elderly man dressed like a Quaker.

In addition to all this there was a heavy old-fashioned bedstead which was constantly being moved into the middle of the room, no matter how many times it was put back. This was witnessed by an Ambulance man who thought he was having his leg pulled when told about it. He was invited in to witness the phenomenon. This he did and is said to have left with a very white face.

Another story from Babbacombe, though taking us back to the middle of the last century, seems to be well authenticated by reliable witnesses. It is quoted in *The Historical Survey of Babbacombe & St Marychurch*, the report was made in 1907 by Dr. Stephenson, a Grimsby Magistrate. He was speaking of an experience which befell him "40 years ago", i.e. in 1867. He related how he came to spend a holiday at Babbacombe with his friend the Rev. Wilson, who was Curate of Babbacombe Church—presumably All Saints. He lived in a small isolated cottage with a housekeeper and a rough-haired terrier for company. The first night of Dr. Stephenson's visit was a very stormy one and a chimney was blown down, collapsing into the bedroom where they were to have slept. As a result a move was made to a small boxroom which Wilson said was haunted. He was later called away to the bedside of a sick parishioner, whilst Stephenson retired to bed on his own. He was awakened after a while by the dog moaning. On looking at him he found that his hair was bristling. He was glaring at the window. On turning round Stephenson was amazed to see the figure of a bluejacket. His shirt was wide open and his chest and garments covered with blood. Over his heart was a terrible gash. He gazed horror-stricken at the apparition who beckoned to him and put his finger into the wound. Stephenson pulled himself together, going towards the sailor. But he stumbled and fell, knowing no more until he found the housekeeper attending to a wound which he had sustained to his cheek when he fell. The visitor told his friend, on his return, that he could stay no longer in the haunted cottage after what had happened, and left the next day.

Shortly afterwards he received a letter from the Rev. Wilson. In it he related how he had had a remarkable statement from the sick man whom he visited on that fatal night. He stated that sixty years ago (i.e. in about 1807) he had been employed in building the cottage in which the Rev. Wilson lived. During the excavations he had unearthed the body of a bluejacket with a deep wound in his chest. Round his neck he wore a handsome gold crucifix. The workman and his mate decided to bury the body, sell the crucifix and say no more about it. This they did, dividing the money. They bricked the body up in the wall of the cottage. But the thing had haunted them for the rest of their lives. Now the old workman lay dying and he hoped they would give the body a Christian burial before he died.

To cut a long story short, that is exactly what happened. The body was found in the thickness of the wall, under the window, in a standing position. It was buried with a church ceremony. Just a few moments after the service, the old workman died.

In Portland Road, Babbacombe, there is a house which formerly had the ghost of a dog. There was lino on the stairs at the time, and each night the footsteps of a dog, which had recently died, was heard to patter up the stairs. When it reached the landing it would be heard to have a good scratch and then patter downstairs. On the arrival of a new puppy, however, the ghost of the old dog disappeared.

A Ghost in a Newspaper Office

A ghost in a newspaper office is quite unusual, but read on and you will learn what happened when the *Herald Express* offices and printing works were built in Barton Hill Road.

It was reported in the *Herald Express* for 19th June 1986 that when the paper's new offices were being built in the late 1970s the skull of a young woman was discovered. The pathologist's report stated that her burial had taken place some two hundred years previously, and the skull was re-interred. It was not stated where. An electrician who was working on the site had a horrible shock not long after this when he saw the head of a dark-haired woman pass through a wall, followed by a low, moaning sigh. Other unexplained sounds were heard at about the same time. Nothing further has been reported, however, but how the woman's skull came to be buried 200 years ago in what would then be a field is something of a mystery.

Tor Hill Road

Mr Bert Blatchford, a carpenter, was carrying out alterations to an old stable situated in a lane which runs behind the properties in Tor Hill Road on the south side of the road. Suddenly he heard a rustling noise like wind. "I looked round," he stated to a *Torquay Times* reporter, "to see what it was and saw a white object about three feet high come out from a corner and disappear into the floor where I had recently boarded up an old staircase. I was absolutely taken aback. I stood there for a while trying to make out what it was when suddenly a large door slammed for no reason at all. There wasn't a breath of wind about and the door must weigh about a hundredweight." Mr Blatchford was alone at the time and added that had it been dark he would have rushed from the building. The object moved like a beam of light, was narrow at the top and thickened out at the bottom. It floated about a foot from the ground. The building, which is thought to be about 150 years old is being converted into a store-room and has been unused for some time.

The Palace Hotel

One of the most notable of the Bishops of Exeter during the nineteenth century was Dr. Henry Phillpotts. His views on church matters were controversial in the extreme, and so unpopular was he at Exeter that he moved out of the Palace and built himself an Italianate villa at Torquay. Here he resided for the rest of his days. The house stood just above Anstey's Cove and some of it still stands as a part of the Palace Hotel. Here it seems that his ghost is seen from time to time. Quoting from the *Herald Express* of 8th November 1978, Mr G. Mitchell, the deputy head porter stated that he had seen the Bishop. "He was standing in front of me," he said, "and as soon as I walked towards him he just melted away and I felt terribly cold." Some of the guests have seen him and so have some of the porters and chambermaids. One housemaid used to keep a dog, but he refused to pass the rooms where the Bishop had lived. "When I saw him," Mr Mitchell continued, "it was as though he was behind a lace curtain, but he was wearing his full regalia, including his hat."

Two More Hotel Hauntings

In St. Marychurch Road, Torquay, not far from the Baptist Church, there is a hotel which is haunted in rather an unusual way. In a ground floor bedroom, for instance, the former proprietress told me that the steady ticking of a large clock is heard from time to time. No reason can be found for this phenomenon.

More disturbing by far was an occasion when she and several friends were in a ground floor room when they heard a terrific crash on the stairs. It sounded as though someone had hurled some heavy piece of furniture, such as a table down the stairwell.They all rushed into the hall to see whatever had happened only to be greeted by ... nothing at all!

When sleeping in a certain bedroom the proprietress said that she frequently heard footsteps on stairs which led to a higher landing.They are the footsteps of a workman in heavy boots. Guests have also commented on this sound. In spite of so many odd occurrences I was assured that the house had a happy atmosphere.

Another hotel where there were psychic disturbances is the Royal Hotel at Babbacombe. During the summer of 1989 the hotel was in the hands of workmen. The *Herald Express* reported that a certain bedroom had a strange atmosphere and none of the workmen would enter it alone. If possible they avoided it. Prior to this one of the staff whilst working in the room was touched by an unseen hand. She declined to enter the room again.

When the hotel was due for re-opening the manager called in the services of a medium who pronounced that the ghost had gone. The manager said that so far nothing further had been reported. A medium told me that there are several hotels in Torbay which are haunted and that he is frequently called in professionally. Hoteliers prefer to get rid of their ghosts!

The "Bull and Bush", Belgrave Road

It was reported in the *Herald Express* in December 1982 that in this pub an inexplicable chill was felt there very often at 11 p.m. This phenomenon was reported by Lynne Walker of Trowbridge. No explanation was forthcoming. Recent enquiries show that this haunting has died out.

Blagdon Inn, Paignton

In the *Sunday Independent* of 22nd January 1978 there was mention of a spook at the Blagdon Inn, Totnes Road, Paignton. The story is that it is haunted by the ghost of a groom who, over a century ago, hanged himself in the stables there. He is known as John Henry, and whether these were his real names or whether they are nicknames, I cannot tell you but I do know that he is extremely sensitive, and if anyone has been deriding his memory, or "taking the mickey" out of him, he becomes extremely active and throws things about. On these occasions bottles are broken, chairs are thrown across the bar, furniture put in the wrong place, coat hangers torn from walls and coats thrown about. An expensive fire also took place after a local comedian had been making fun of John Henry. It is thought that he started the blaze in his rage.

Enquiries made at the Blagdon Inn recently reveal that John Henry has never been seen, but his presence is still felt and things get moved inexplicably.

The Prince Regent (The Inn on the Green)

There is a really friendly ghost in the cellar of a pub in Paignton, formerly known as the "Prince Regent", but now the "Inn on the Green". He sometimes comes upstairs to sit on the children's beds. They are not in the least upset by him. Mrs Mudge, who at the time of a newspaper report was the wife of the licensee, said she saw him sometimes like a blur and could walk through him. There used to be an old brick tower attached to the hotel, and Alfred, as he is called, "lived" there. When the tower was demolished he moved into the cellar of the hotel. He interferes with the gas pressures which control the beer, switches lights on and off and also record players, and is generally mischievous. Paddy Hanna, the caretaker, once had the fright of his life when he actually saw the bolts to the cellar door being drawn back by hands which he could not see. The children love him, however, and used to leave him Christmas cards at the top of the cellar steps. A medium when called in contacted him; he said that his name was Alfred and that he had been hanged at the age of 31 during the Napoleonic Wars. His crime was unknown.

The pub has changed its name to the "Inn on the Green" since the time of the above report which dated from 8th June 1976. Recent enquiries there show that Alfred is still very active. Several of the waiters and barmen whom I interviewed were only

too convinced of his existence. These included Kevin, David Richardson and Mark Bellworthy to mention only a few. All had witnessed glasses being pushed along the shelf in the main bar, whilst a light under the counter which is never used was switched on and off. None of the waiters would go down to the cellar alone if they could avoid it. Here interference with gas pressures and switches still continued. Some had been touched on the shoulder and all had seen beer barrels rocked by an invisible force. Mrs Mary Wynne, a cleaner, testified that one morning at about 8 a.m. she had just arrived and was standing behind the bar when someone touched her on the shoulder as they walked past and said, "Hullo, darling." On turning round to see who it was she saw no one. At the same time she was conscious of a blast of cold air. This phenomenon of cold air often occurs.

It was pointed out to me that the cellar is old, being a part of a house which looks to date from 1860-70. It would not go back so far as the Napoleonic Wars, however, as this part of the Green was under water at that time, and part of a lagoon. So the mystery as to why Albert has found a home at this particular pub remains.

Polsham Villa, Southfield Road

An interesting haunting in Southfield Road is mentioned in the *Western Morning News* for 9th May 1983, and in the *Torbay Times* of 18th July 1985. The house, formerly Polsham Villa and now "Oldway Links Hotel", was built in 1820 but succeeds an even older house on the same site.

In the first newspaper it was reported that there was the ghost of a former nanny there. She was said to go about calling "Master John, Master John." The later report, however, is not nearly so innocuous. At that time the proprietor was being driven distracted by a series of disturbing paranormal events, and the Vicar of Preston had been called in to exorcise the house. The proprietor had watched whilst his bedroom window crashed to the ground for no apparent reason, whilst bath taps would turn themselves on, flooding the kitchen below. He also witnessed two cars back of their own accord into the garage door, whilst a strong ladder collapsed beneath the weight of his young son.

Recent enquiries at Oldway Links find the hotel under different management. The present proprietor told me that after a year at the hotel she has found nothing

unpleasant there. Footsteps have been heard, however, in an old building outside, but whether these are echoes from the street is uncertain. There is something on the top floor also which makes one want to hurry away, and the Manageress told me that every night when she closes the fire door she has this feeling.

Paignton Police Station

It is all very well to demolish a house, but if it had its ghost then that phenomenon has often been noted to reappear in the new building on the old site. This is what seems to have occurred at Paignton Police Station.

According to newspaper reports between 1978 and 1985 Paignton Police Station had a very active ghost and many occult happenings were taking place. Piecing the story together, it seems that the Police Station was built on the site of a former house which was demolished in the 1960s. Here many years ago an old lady had lived, and it is her ghost which is at the bottom of the disturbance. She has been heard by women but is only seen by men. She is dressed in black. Mrs Nora Simms of East Allington, wrote to the *Herald Express* to say that she and her husband had lived in the house for 16 years. They heard her frequently and her husband often saw her. She was friendly and never frightened anyone—in fact they grew quite fond of her and her

ginger cat, which also appeared. The Simmses had a kitchen help who had worked for the old lady and a photograph which she produced tallied with the figure which Mr Simms had seen. Reports as to the old lady's end are conflicting, for whilst Mrs Simms says she did not commit suicide or anything like that, yet another report says that she did, and that is why her unquiet spirit haunts this particular spot.

The old lady caused no trouble to anyone until her house was demolished to make way for the new Police Station. At the time of the demolition she is said to have been seen leaving the building. When the new Police Station was completed, however, she came back with a vengeance. A police constable saw her sitting on a chair in the lounge. He said she looked weird with long hair and staring eyes. This was at one a.m. An Inspector saw her in the men's living quarters and soon after all the papers on his desk flew into the air and were scattered. She was also responsible for papers being hurled across the room, whilst windows were opened and closed, lights switched on and off, and electric kettles boiled. A barman from the social club once brushed against her on the stairs. His arm turned ice cold.

The story of the haunted Police Station hit the headlines in June 1978 and was reported as far away as the U.S.A. and Sweden.

Recent enquiries have produced an assurance from the Superintendent of Police that all is now quiet, and the old lady has not been seen or felt or heard for some time.

Phenomena at Goodrington

Occupying a small promontory in the middle of Goodrington Beach stands Goodrington House. It was built as a hospital for sailors during the Napoleonic Wars. Behind it was a small cemetery of which only one grave now remains. The property is now known as Quaywest Beach Resort and has many water attractions and a restaurant. On Hallowe'en 1988 I did a ghost watch there with Mr L. Sawyer and Mike Trebble, a chef at Quaywest. He told me that at about 1.30 a.m. in the second week of July, he was sitting in his office at a table, when two doors outside the office, and separated from it by a wood partition, opened and closed. The office door then did the same. No one else was there. Later on, in October, he heard a woman's voice about a foot from his ear say, "Mary". He judged her to be the height of his shoulder.

This was at 11 a.m.

Not long ago the house was divided into holiday flats. Guests often mentioned that there was a heavy smell of soup in the atmosphere at about one a.m.

Mr Trebble, when alone, often feels a sense of heaviness in the air and pressure on his temples. A chef who works evenings once heard metallic taps in the kitchen—the sort of noise a knife might make, but there was no one there. A guard dog is reported to refuse to go up one of the staircases.

I expected to hear more of this haunting before long. I was right, for Mr Trebble told me on the phone, as I was writing this, that footsteps have been heard lately in the kitchen and overhead. He also told me that last thing at night he pushes any bills from the evening's takings under the office door, which, of course, is locked. In the morning these have sometimes been found pushed back again into the passage.

But a much older haunting than all these is that of a nun who is at times seen at night behind the house, near the old cemetery, which was used in the times of the Napoleonic Wars. So Goodrington has quite a variety of hauntings on offer.

Kirkham Cottage

This charming thatched cottage must be one of the oldest in Paignton, and its stalwart oak beams are a delight to see. There is poltergeist activity in the kitchen where trays are thrown about from time to time, Nothing has been seen, however, and the activity only occurs when the kitchen is empty.

Blagdon Manor, Near Paignton

Blagdon Manor is situated not very far from the last haunting. It was the mediaeval home of the Kirkhams, who have such a spectacular chantry in Paignton Parish Church. Mrs V. Williams related to me in October 1988 how, when staying at Blagdon Manor, she had been disturbed at night as soon as she put out her light. She felt there were monks moving constantly up and down in the corridor outside. She also saw, each night, at a window opposite her own, a light which would grow in intensity and then diminish. This window was in an unoccupied wing of the house and no explanation was forthcoming. One day she saw, by daylight. a female blackbird in her bedroom which seemed to appear from nowhere. It circled the room for a couple of minutes and then disappeared. No windows or doors were open. The proprietress said it had been seen before.

Mrs Williams then spent a whole night in trying to help the unquiet spirit which she felt to be there. Her vigil, inducing love and peace was successful, for it changed the whole atmosphere; in the morning there was a great sense of peace. Strangely, when she went outside, she saw on the ground a dead female blackbird.

Mrs Williams's mother, Mrs Wrigley, also stayed at Blagdon, but in a different wing. In her room she heard monks chanting at night; also a rushing sound would be heard. Each morning a certain picture which she had brought with her was always askew. This she would straighten each day, but with the same result next morning.

Brixham

People are often shy of speaking of occult experiences which they have had, or of telling you that they live in a haunted house. Perhaps that may be the reason why I have only two hauntings to report at Brixham. So perhaps the reader, now he has got almost to the end of the book, may feel inspired to go to Brixham to see what more occult tales await discovery.

There is a haunting at Brixham of great interest which seems to have continued for as long as people can remember. Unfortunately the owner of the house has been plagued by ghost hunters from every direction, and as a result refuses to discuss the haunting with anyone. I am therefore not able to divulge the position of the house nor yet its name. This situation, however, does not detract from the facts already well known, and indeed published in more than one book. They are presumed to be reasonably accurate, but I have not been able to check them.

Quite unlike the case of "Castel-a-Mare" in Torquay, we have here a good reason for the hauntings—a double suicide committed on the same day. The sad story is that long ago the lord of the manor was a certain Squire Hilliard who lived in the house concerned. His son unfortunately fell in love with a country maid from Churston, and his father strongly objected to a marriage. So it was arranged that the young lady should marry someone of her own class. It chanced that the squire's son was riding past the church at the time of her wedding, and what should he see but his beloved coming out of the church on the arm of another man. The luckless lover, overcome with grief, went immediately and hanged himself, leaving his horse to find its own way home, riderless. When the sad news was broken to Squire Hilliard, he was filled with remorse at what he had caused and also made away with himself.

The ghost of a man in old-fashioned dress has been frequently seen after dark at an upstairs window, the room appearing to be lighted. This is said to be the Squire, and apparently during the last war he caused much alarm to a passing policeman who immediately informed the surprised householder that the blackout regulations were being infringed. There are also footsteps—some stealthy and subdued, but others are loud and heavy. They are heard in particular near the staircase. Then there are, on occasion, loud bangs, creaks and rhythmic tappings. A moaning or sighing sound seems to coincide with the full moon. Doors lock and unlock themselves, and the occupier has been both locked out of the house and locked in various rooms.

A common sound is the clatter of a horse's hooves, which comes from the lawn. Some digging was done here and I am told that an old cobbled courtyard was laid bare. So is this ghost sound set up by the hooves of the unfortunate lover's horse returning riderless to its stable after its master had hanged himself?

This house is obviously of considerable age, and could succeed another even older one which once stood on the same site.

The Three Elms

In Drew Street is a pub, the "Three Elms", which has the ghost of an old man which some have seen. Footsteps are often heard on the stairs and screaming has also been recorded. The house, which goes back some centuries, is said to have a creepy feel about it, and some will not be there alone.

Recent enquiries show nothing to report except the switching on and off of light switches.

Royal Castle Hotel, Dartmouth

The Royal Castle Hotel at Dartmouth is much older than it appears, and parts of it are said to date back to the close of the sixteenth century at least. There is an association with Charles II, who is said to have off-loaded his unwanted mistresses here. After arriving there, one was never seen again. Is it the rattle of her coach and four, as it drives into the cobbled yard of this old inn which is still heard?

Lesley Park, in an article written for the *Gazette* in November 1979 tells how she visited the hotel with a purpose in mind—to sleep in the haunted bedroom, with its reputed priest's hole. She stayed awake until 2.30 a.m. but as nothing untoward had occurred she settled down to sleep. Not for long, however, for she was soon shaken out of her sleep by an unseen hand, and at the same time was conscious of being icy cold and shivering. But no one was to be seen. Later she was kept awake by a thumping sound, the cause of which she could not discover. Eventually it became more and more agitated, and finally she felt the bed shaken. At 5 a.m. her alarm clock, set for 7 a.m., went off. She re-set it and tried to get some sleep, but the clock went off again. In all it rang three times before 7 a.m.

On beginning to dress next morning she found that the ghost had moved an article of clothing and put it on the other side of the room by the priest's hole. It was her bra!

Recent enquiries confirm that the old cobbled courtyard is now under cover and is the main foyer of the hotel. In fact the paranormal activities there are so persistent that a night porter has recently relinquished his job in that part of the building.

This then concludes my collection of the ghost stories of Torbay so far. I expect several have escaped my notice. Then again, quite a few people will have experienced paranormal activities but are perhaps too shy to mention them. In this way many interesting happenings may be lost for all time. I do ask such people to get in touch with me so that a future edition of this book may be twice the size.